Healthy Me

STAY FIT

Your Guide to Staying Active

By Sara Hunt

Consultant:
Nicole Cormier, RD, LDN
Delicious Living Nutrition Online
Middleboro, MA

CAPSTONE PRESS
a capstone imprint

Snap Books are published by Capstone Press,
151 Good Counsel Drive, P.O. Box 669, Mankato, Minnesota 56002.
www.capstonepub.com

Books published by Capstone Press are manufactured with paper
containing at least 10 percent post-consumer waste.

Library of Congress Cataloging-in-Publication Data
Hunt, Sara.
  Stay fit : your guide to staying active / by Sara Hunt.
    p. cm. — (Snap books. healthy me.)
  Includes bibliographical references and index.
  Summary: "Provides tips on exercise, diet, and general fitness"—Provided by publisher.
  ISBN 978-1-4296-6545-2 (library binding)
  ISBN 978-1-4296-7293-1 (paperback)
  1. Physical fitness—Handbooks, manuals, etc. 2. Exercise—Handbooks, manuals, etc.
3. Health—Handbooks, manuals, etc. I. Title.
  RA781.H797 2012
  613.7'1—dc22   2011007408

Editor: Mari Bolte
Designer: Juliette Peters
Media Researcher: Svetlana Zhurkin
Production Specialist: Laura Manthe

Photo Credits
Alamy: Myrleen Pearson, 19; Capstone Studio: Karon Dubke, 7, 9, 12, 14, 15, 17, 18 (bottom), 21 (both), 22, 24, 25, 27, 29; Corbis: David Stoecklein, 8; Dreamstime: Alexander Rochau, 20, Greg Da Silva, 11; Shutterstock: Africa Studio, cover (top left), Elena Elisseeva, 13, Elnur, cover (bottom left), Jason Stitt, cover (front), Ken Hurst, 18 (top), Maksym Blazej, 23, maxstockphoto, cover (right), Shawn Pecor, 5, Sonya Etchison, 26

Essential content terms are **bold** and are defined at the bottom of the page where they first appear.

Printed in the United States of America in North Mankato, Minnesota.
032011   006110CGF11

Table of Contents

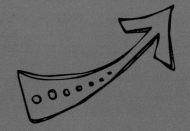

Chapter 1

Making the Right Choice

Wake Up Right

BEEEEP! Your alarm goes off. You hit the snooze button and pull the covers over your head. You stayed up late watching a movie again, and you're paying for it now! Finally, you get up, take a quick shower, and hurry to eat your breakfast. You live just a few blocks from school, but you catch a ride with your dad.

The best part of your day is gym. Your class is playing soccer, your favorite sport. Running after the ball makes you tired, though. Your classmates seem to have plenty of energy. Why do you feel so worn out?

You walk home after school. When you get home, you snag some microwave popcorn while Skyping with your friend. Then it's time to get started on your homework. It's still light out when you finish, but you decide to catch up on your TV shows. You sit in front of the DV-R while you wait for dinner.

After dinner, your brother wants help playing his new video game. "Just for a minute," you say. Three hours later, you're still playing. Where did the time go?

Later, while in bed, you think back on the day. Your gym teacher said that everyone should get an hour of exercise each day. You were busy, but you don't feel like you got that much physical activity. What could you have done differently?

Chapter 2

Control Your Day

Get Moving!

Take a look at your daily schedule. It probably feels like you're on autopilot. Sleep. Eat. School. Repeat. You spend between six and seven hours a day at school and eight hours sleeping. That leaves less than 10 hours for everything else you need to get done. But being out and about isn't always the same as being active. Get creative! You can find ways to fit in one hour of physical activity. There's no rule that says your hour has to be done all at once.

If you have gym class for 30 minutes each day, you're halfway to your goal! Walk with a friend for 15 minutes, and you're only 15 minutes away. You can find lots of fun ways to make up the difference. Take the stairs, skateboard to a friend's house, or work out while watching TV. Try to exercise most days of the week. As long as your time equals 60 minutes a day, you'll be in good shape!

Start with a plan. Get excited about regular activity. A good time to exercise is right after school. Instead of reaching for the remote, head outside. Ride your bike, play catch with a friend, or take a walk around the block. Keeping your body fit will help you feel recharged and ready to take on your homework. There may even be time left over for a little TV afterward!

Healthy Tip

Try to exercise before doing anything else. You're less likely to get moving once you're in front of the TV or computer.

Too Much Technology?

Technology makes our lives easier in many ways. But the time you spend checking your e-mail, texting, or reading status updates is time spent not moving your body.

It's easy to flip on the TV or surf the Web. But the next time you're bored, try something active! Shoot some hoops or learn to skateboard. If you really want to watch a show or play a video game, make a deal with yourself. If you spend 30 minutes watching TV, spend another 30 doing something active.

Technology can make your workout more fun. Plug into your iPod and get moving to your favorite tunes. Dance along with a music video or copy the stars' moves in your favorite musical. Download an app or Podcast that has fitness or nutrition tips. Got a long-distance friend? Try doing yoga together over Skype.

Just the Facts

In a 2010 survey, the average American spent 2.8 hours a day watching TV. Kids between the ages of 15 and 19 spent an additional hour playing video games or using the computer.

Sweat It for 60

To get the most out of your physical activity, make sure you're getting at least 60 minutes of moderate or vigorous exercise a day.

Physical Activities

Activity	Type	Speed
walking	moderate	3.5 miles (5.6 kilometers) per hour (or 100 steps per minute)
	vigorous	4.5 miles (7.2 km) per hour
bicycling	moderate	less than 10 miles (16 km) per hour
	vigorous	more than 10 miles per hour
jogging/running	vigorous	5 miles (8 km) per hour
ice skating	moderate	9 miles (14.5 km) per hour
cross-country skiing	moderate	less than 5 miles (8 km) per hour
	vigorous	more than 5 miles per hour

You should be able to talk comfortably during moderate physical activity. Your breathing rate will increase, but it should be deep and regular. If you are gasping for air or feel short of breath, slow down.

Some physical activities, such as light housework, normal walking, or shopping, don't count toward your 60 minutes a day. If an activity does not raise your heart rate, it can't count toward your goal. But that doesn't mean you shouldn't do them. Any activity is better than no activity.

vigorous—something done at an intense pace

Chapter 3

Healthy Body, Healthy Mind!

Why is it so important to be active? Regular exercise helps boost **metabolism**, increase muscle, and reduce body fat. Your extra energy will also improve your mood and help you think more clearly.

Your body is always using energy. It even needs energy when you sleep! Metabolism turns **calories** from food into energy or fuel. That helps your body function. Physical activity increases your metabolism both during and after exercise.

metabolism—the way our bodies process food

calorie—the amount of energy that food gives you

Proteins, **carbohydrates**, and fats are nutrients that give your body energy. Different foods have different amounts of these nutrients. The nutrients have different amounts of calories, and so make different amounts of energy.

protein—a substance found in foods such as meat, cheese, eggs, and fish

carbohydrate—a nutrient that provides energy

Just the Facts

The National Academy of Sciences recommends that 45 to 60 percent of your daily calories come from carbohydrates. Carbohydrates include fruit, vegetables, dairy, and grains. However, a 2010 study revealed that 40 percent of kids' calories come from baked goods, pizza, and soda.

The first key to keeping a healthy body is balancing your energy in and energy out. Energy in comes from the calories you get by eating and drinking. Energy out equals the calories you burn by exercising. To stay healthy, your energy out should be equal to or greater than your energy in.

Being physically active when you're young will help you later in life. A healthy body today reduces the chance of heart disease, high blood pressure, and other dangerous conditions later in life.

There are other advantages too. Regular exercise can increase your attention span, which can help you stay focused at school. It raises your energy level and helps you sleep more soundly.

The second key to a healthy body is getting enough protein and **fiber**. Protein and fiber work together to keep your body working correctly. Getting enough of these nutrients will help you feel full and alert. Protein can be found in fruits, vegetables, meat, and dairy. Fiber is found in vegetables, fruits, and whole grains. Making sure your body has the right nutrients will help you stay healthy.

fiber—a nutrient that helps your body digest food

Chapter 4

New Ways to Move

Trying new things can improve your body's health. Variety will keep your body alert and your mind fresh. Pro football players have tried yoga, mixed martial arts, and even ballet. They found that cross-training helped them play better on the field. It works for them, and it can work for you!

Activities, such as kickboxing, pilates, and zumba, provide a workout with both moderate and vigorous movements. They enhance strength and flexibility. They also use many different muscle groups.

Want to go for a triple play? Try soccer, brisk walking, or in-line skating. These activities improve endurance, strength, and flexibility. Some other sports that improve all three are tennis, swimming, dancing, and ice skating.

If you'd like to try a new sport, go for it! You can practice basic skills for soccer or basketball right in your own backyard. Check the Internet to find a place that teaches horseback riding. These activities use different muscle groups. Or talk your friends into going to a yoga class at the local gym or studio. You might feel more comfortable if you're with someone you know.

Not interested in trying out for the team? You can be active on your own. Try aerobics or swimming laps. Even doing chores can be good exercise, as long as you're raising your heart rate. Raking leaves, washing the car, or mowing the lawn can get you moving. Make a game of it by tracking your steps with a pedometer. Try to walk 2 miles (3.2 kilometers) each day. That's about 10,000 steps.

Just the Facts

More than 40 million kids in the United States participate in organized sports. However, only one-fourth of them reach 60 minutes of moderate or vigorous exercise during practice.

If you have one, a dog can be a great exercise buddy. Take a walk. Visit an agility course. Have a race! You won't just be spending time with your pup. You'll be getting some much-needed physical activity too.

It's true that video games can get a bad rap. But some games are better than others. Games that encourage movement can be a fun way to get you off the couch. Some use fast-paced dance steps. Others copy the moves used in boxing, skiing, or running. Remember, it doesn't count if you don't get off the couch.

Endurance, Strength, and Flexibility

Your physical fitness can be measured by endurance, strength, and flexibility. Each one is important to your overall body health. Not being active can lower your body's energy and fitness over time.

Endurance measures your **stamina** and heart health. Regular physical activity at a moderate or vigorous pace can increase your endurance. Try running, bicycling, rowing, or swimming.

stamina—the energy and strength to keep doing something for a long time

Strength measures your muscle tone. Your body builds muscle tone through strength conditioning. Building muscle increases the number of calories you burn. Exercises like sit-ups, curl-ups, and weight lifting can help increase your strength.

Flexibility measures your body's ability to bend, reach, and stretch. Stretching is an easy and effective way to improve flexibility. You can also try hip-hop dancing, karate, or swimming.

Chapter 5

Play It Safe

Being active has its benefits. But with any activity, there are a few risks. By training correctly and using the right equipment, you can reduce the chance of injury. Stretch well before and after your workout. Know your limits. You wouldn't run a marathon after your first track practice, would you?

Some sports have specific gear designed for your safety. Football and hockey players wear helmets and pads to protect them from injury. Horseback riders wear helmets and boots. Other sports use shin guards, goggles, face masks, or mouth guards.

Even if safety gear isn't a part of your chosen activity, it's important to wear proper gear. There's a reason wrestlers, runners, and gymnasts wear tight-fitting clothes. Try not to wear baggy clothes that could get caught on things.

Believe it or not, the most important piece of equipment for almost any activity protects your feet. A pair of quality, properly-fitted shoes or cleats are key. Make sure they have good support. Check that the bottoms aren't too worn. And make sure they're a good fit for the sport of your choice.

Before starting your workout, there's one final thing you'll need. It's water! Get yourself a reusable bottle, and keep water with you all the time. Feeling thirsty is a sign of **dehydration**, so don't wait to take a drink.

Want something with a little flavor? Try a sports drink. Many sports drinks are mostly water with some added **electrolytes**. You may find it easier to stay hydrated with sports drinks than with regular water. But watch out—sports drinks have around 50 to 60 calories per 8-ounce (240-milliliter) serving. They can also have lots of sugar.

Healthy Tip

If you have a sweet tooth, add a bit of 100 percent juice to your water bottle.

dehydration—the condition that occurs when the body does not have enough water

electrolyte—a mineral that encourages the body to drink more water

Physical activity in extreme heat can be dangerous. If you're outside on a hot day, make sure you don't get too hot. When your body gets overheated, you can get **heatstroke**. Take breaks, sit in the shade, and pour water on your head to cool off.

heatstroke—a serious illness caused by exercising in the heat too long

It's important to get enough water before, during, and after workouts. Weigh yourself before and after exercising to determine how much weight you lost while working out. That way you'll know how much water to drink afterward.

2 hours before working out:
8–16 ounces (240–480 mL) of water

30 minutes before working out:
8–16 oz. of water

15 minutes after you start your workout:
3–6 oz. (90–180 mL) of water

30 minutes after you start your workout:
3–6 oz. of water

45 minutes after you start your workout:
3–6 oz. of water

After working out:
8–16 oz. of water for every pound you have lost while working out

Go for the Goal!

Now that you've got some tips on keeping fit, make a plan to get moving! Set personal goals for yourself. What can you do today? What can you do this week? What about the not-so-distant future? Here are a few simple tips for setting your own goals.

- **Be realistic:** Your goals should be challenging but reasonable. Keep your age, fitness level, and experience in mind when setting your goals.
- **Think short term:** Choose goals that you can reach in the near future.
- **Keep it simple:** Goals should be simple. Pick one major behavior to change.

- **Track your progress:** Keep an activity log or chart. Write down each time you are physically active.
- **Put it in writing:** Write down your goals and put them somewhere you can see them every day. Some examples of fitness goals might be:
    - I will play soccer with my friends for 60 minutes each day for a week.
    - I will increase my activity time by 15 minutes each week until I reach 60 minutes a day.
    - Each week, I will spend two days practicing a new activity. For example, my jump shot or a new dance routine.

Slow and Steady Wins the Race!

Don't expect to change your habits overnight. It takes time to establish a new routine. Before you start any new activity, it's a good idea to talk with your doctor. This is especially important if you're overweight, have an old injury, or have any sort of medical condition. Your doctor will let you know if your exercise program is right for you.

Find a starting point. When you're ready, slowly increase the intensity and amount of activity over a period of time. Listen to your body. Slow down if you're tired or something hurts. Speed up or push harder if it feels too easy. And remember, change doesn't happen overnight. A friend or family member can help you stay on track and focused.

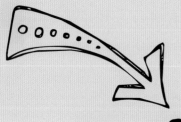

Healthy Tip

Figure out how much weekly exercise you get. Increase the level of activity a little bit each week. But keep the increase under 10 percent. You don't want to wear yourself out or risk injury.

Celebrate Success!

Any amount of change or progress in your goal to get moving is reason to celebrate. If you stick to it, you will begin to see results in both mind and body. Whatever your goal is, be proud of yourself for making the effort to move your body. The result will show in the healthiest you possible!

Glossary

calorie (KA-luh-ree)—a measurement of the amount of energy that food gives you

carbohydrate (kar-boh-HYE-drate)—sugars, starches, and fiber; a major source of energy for humans

dehydration (dee-hy-DRAY-shuhn)—a condition that occurs when the body does not have enough water

electrolyte (i-lek-TRAH-lyte)—a mineral that encourages the body to drink more water; electrolytes contain an electric charge

fiber (FY-buhr)—a nutrient that helps your body digest food

heatstroke (HEET-strohk)—a serious illness caused by working or exercising in the heat too long

metabolism (muh-TAH-buhl-ism)—the way our bodies make use of the food we eat

protein (PROH-teen)—a substance found in all living plant and animal cells; foods such as meat, cheese, eggs, beans, and fish are sources of dietary protein

stamina (STAM-uh-nuh)—the energy and strength to keep doing something for a long time

vigorous (vi-GUH-russ)—something done at an intense pace

Read More

Hunt, Jamie. *Getting Stronger, Getting Fit: The Importance of Exercise.* Kids & Obesity. Broomall, Penn.: Mason Crest Publishers, 2010.

Kajander, Rebecca, and Timothy Culbert. *Be Fit, Be Strong, Be You.* Be the Boss of Your Body. Minneapolis, Minn.: Free Spirit Pub., 2010.

Rau, Dana Meachan. *Fitness For Fun!* For Fun. Minneapolis: Compass Point Books, 2009.

Internet Sites

FactHound offers a safe, fun way to find Internet sites related to this book. All of the sites on FactHound have been researched by our staff.

Here's all you do:

Visit *www.facthound.com*

Type in this code: 9781429665452

Check out projects, games and lots more at **www.capstonekids.com**

Index

activities, 4, 6, 8, 10, 11, 16, 18, 19, 20, 21, 27

calories, 12, 13, 14, 21, 24
carbohydrates, 13

dehydration, 24

electrolytes, 24
endurance, 16, 20
energy, 12, 13, 14, 20
equipment, 22, 23

fats, 13
fiber, 15
fitness, 20–21, 26
flexibility, 16, 20, 21

goals, 6, 11, 26–27, 28, 29

heart health, 14, 20
heart rate, 11, 18
heatstroke, 25

injuries, 22, 25, 28

metabolism, 12

National Academy of Sciences, 13
nutrients, 13, 15

protein, 13, 15

safety, 22, 23
stamina, 20
strength, 16, 20, 21
stretching, 21

technology, 4, 8, 9, 16, 19

video games, 4, 9, 19

water, 24, 25